HARDCOURT

HARDCOURT

STORIES FROM 75 YEARS OF THE

NATIONAL BASKETBALL ASSOCIATION

BY **FRED BOWEN**

ILLUSTRATED BY

JAMES E. RANSOME

MARGARET K. McELDERRY BOOKS

NEW YORK   LONDON   TORONTO   SYDNEY   NEW DELHI

ALSO BY FRED BOWEN
AND JAMES E. RANSOME

GRIDIRON

MARGARET K. McELDERRY BOOKS • An imprint of Simon & Schuster Children's Publishing Division • 1230 Avenue of the Americas, New York, New York 10020 • Text copyright © 2022 by Fred Bowen • Illustrations copyright © 2022 by James Ransome • All rights reserved, including the right of reproduction in whole or in part in any form. • MARGARET K. McELDERRY BOOKS is a trademark of Simon & Schuster, Inc. • For information about special discounts for bulk purchases, please contact Simon & Schuster Special Sales at 1-866-506-1949 or business@simonandschuster.com. • The Simon & Schuster Speakers Bureau can bring authors to your live event. For more information or to book an event, contact the Simon & Schuster Speakers Bureau at 1-866-248-3049 or visit our website at www.simonspeakers.com. • The text for this book was set in Arno Pro. • The illustrations for this book were rendered in watercolor. • Manufactured in China • 1021 SCP • First Edition • 10 9 8 7 6 5 4 3 2 1 • Library of Congress Cataloging-in-Publication Data • Names: Bowen, Fred, author. | Ransome, James, illustrator. • Title: Hardcourt : stories from 75 years of the National Basketball Association / by Fred Bowen ; illustrated by James E. Ransome. • Description: First edition. | New York : Margaret K. McElderry Books, [2022] | Includes bibliographical references and index. | Audience: Ages 8–12. | Audience: Grades 4–6. | Summary: "The story of the National Basketball Association from its origins through the major events and players who made basketball what it is today"—Provided by publisher. • Identifiers: LCCN 2021020739 (print) | LCCN 2021020740 (ebook) | ISBN 9781534460430 (hardcover) | ISBN 9781534460447 (ebook) • Subjects: LCSH: National Basketball Association—Juvenile literature. | Basketball—United States—History—Juvenile literature. | Basketball players—United States—Juvenile literature. • Classification: LCC GV885.1.B673 2022 (print) | LCC GV885.1 (ebook) | DDC 796.323/6406—dc23 • LC record available at https://lccn.loc.gov/2021020739 • LC ebook record available at https://lccn.loc.gov/2021020740

THE TIP-OFF

It started after World War II with a bunch of empty sports arenas. Too many days and nights when there were no games, and the bright lights were off and everything was dark.

Places such as the old Madison Square Garden on 8th Avenue between 49th and 50th streets in Manhattan. The Boston Garden at North Station. The Philadelphia Arena and Chicago Stadium. The Duquesne Gardens in Pittsburgh and the Uline Arena in northeast Washington, D.C.

The owners of these places knew one simple truth—you can't make any money when no one is in the building. You have to have some attraction that makes people want to show up.

There was always the circus. Ice shows were big. Boxing was popular in the 1940s, especially the heavyweights. Everyone knew Joe Louis. Pro wrestling, bicycle races, anything to draw a crowd. Some of the owners had teams in the National Hockey League.

But they needed more. The soldiers were coming home from Europe and the Pacific. They were buying houses, starting families, and looking for ways to spend their money and have some fun. Maybe forget about the horrors of the war—seventy million dead, including more than four hundred thousand Americans.

Maybe the arena owners could try another professional sport. Baseball was king back then. People couldn't wait to see Ted Williams and Joe DiMaggio swing the bat again. Horse racing was big too, but you can't race horses inside. The National Football League had been around for more than twenty years, although you would hardly know it. The NFL was not that big a deal in 1946.

College basketball was drawing more crowds in some cities. The National Invitational Tournament (NIT) was a big event in New York. Maybe a professional basketball league would work. The National Basketball League (NBL) had been in business for a while. Mostly around the Midwest and in small towns such as Hammond, Indiana; Sheboygan, Wisconsin; and Youngstown, Ohio.

So they gave it a try. Called the new league the Basketball Association of America (BAA). They started with eleven teams the first year. They played a sixty-game schedule in front of a lot of empty seats. But at least the arenas weren't completely empty.

And slowly . . . it wasn't easy . . . the league got bigger. There was something about the game and the players that made people sit up and notice. Players such as George Mikan, Bob Cousy, Bill Russell, Bob Pettit, and Wilt Chamberlain. Hard not to notice Wilt. He was listed at seven feet, one inch tall, and 275 pounds.

But the story of professional basketball is a long one. Seventy-five years of hardcourt history. How a game that started in a YMCA gymnasium in Springfield, Massachusetts, grew into the biggest and best basketball league in the world.

The NBA.

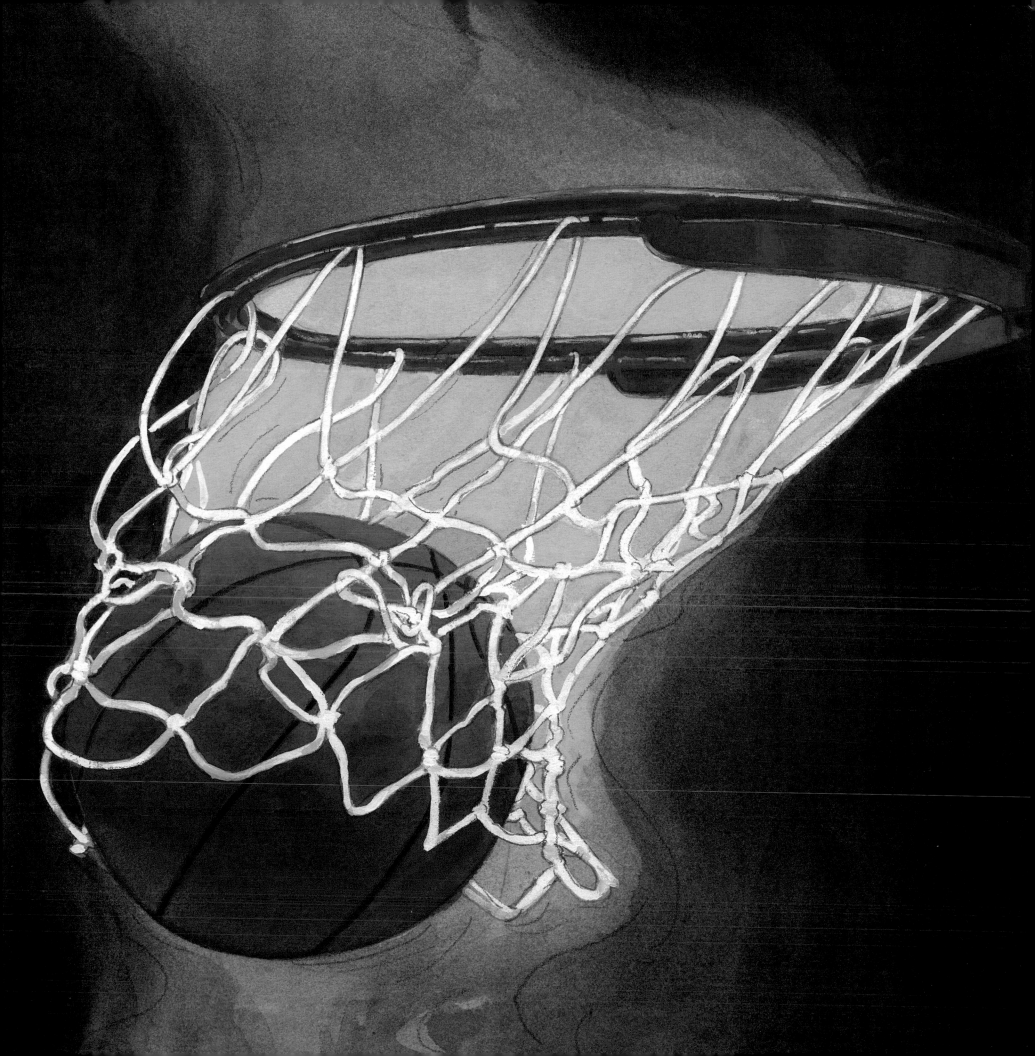

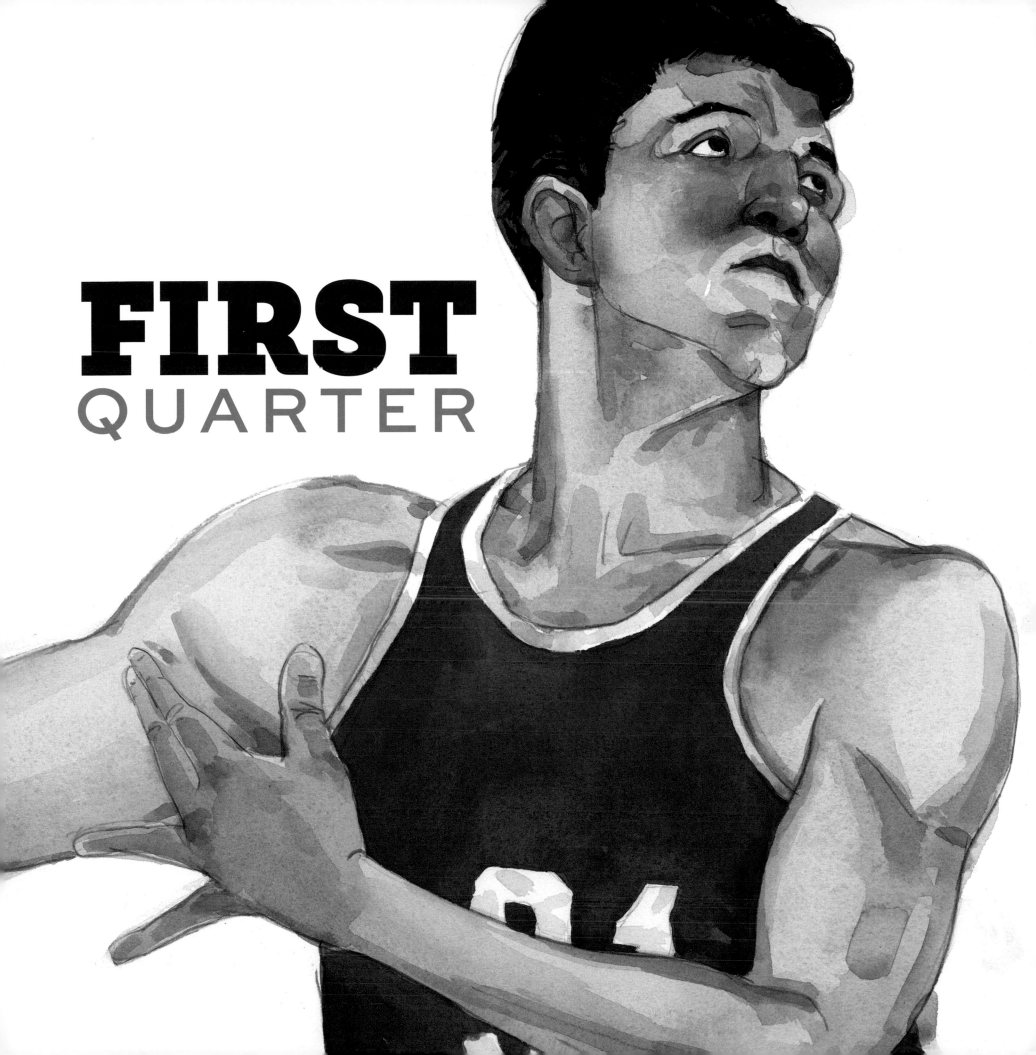

ONE

A NEW GAME

James Naismith had to come up with something . . . quick. Or he might be out of a job.

The thirty-year-old physical education instructor at the International YMCA Training School in Springfield, Massachusetts, had a class of eighteen restless boys. It was December 1891 and too cold to go outside and play football or baseball. Tempers were running short.

The school's directors told Naismith to come up with a game that would give the boys some exercise. But not break anything or any bones in the gym.

They gave Naismith two weeks.

Two weeks later, Naismith had the school's janitor, Pop Stebbins, nail a peach basket at each end of the gymnasium. The baskets were ten feet above the floor and secured to a railing that ran along the edge of the gym balcony. There were no backboards.

Naismith then asked Mrs. Lyons, the secretary at the school, to type up the thirteen rules for his new game. The idea of the game was for the players to throw the ball—a soccer ball—into one of the peach baskets. Some of the rules stated:

- The ball may be thrown in any direction with one or both hands.
- The ball may be batted in any direction with one or both hands (never with the fist).
- A player cannot run with the ball. The player must throw it from the spot on which he catches it. . . .

7

- No shouldering, holding, pushing, tripping, or striking in any way the person of an opponent . . . .

Finally, the rules declared:

- The time shall be two fifteen-minute halves, with five minutes' rest between.
- The side making the most goals in that time shall be declared the winner. . . .

When the eighteen boys arrived at the YMCA on December 21, 1891, Naismith divided them into two teams. As Naismith recalled years later in an interview:

"There were three forwards, three centers, and three backs on each team. I chose two of the center men to jump, then threw the ball between them. It was the start of the first basketball game and the finish of the trouble with that class."

That first game of basketball was different from today's game. For example, there was no dribbling. The players just passed the ball among themselves. And, although Naismith did not want a rough game, eighteen players in a small Springfield gym (fifty feet by thirty-five feet) meant that there was plenty of rough stuff.

The first game was low scoring. The contest ended with a score of 1–0. William R. Chase made the first and only goal by tossing the ball into the peach basket from half court.

The boys wanted to call the new game "Naismith ball" in honor of their teacher. Naismith preferred another name . . . basket ball. The two words were joined into one word years later.

The game caught on quickly in YMCAs and gyms around the country. Naismith's game changed as the players experimented with the rules. For example, players began to dribble the ball to move around the court. Backboards (made of chicken wire!) first appeared in 1893. The peach baskets disappeared around the same time.

The rules were changed later so that a basket counted for two points and players were awarded foul shots after fouls. Games were played with different numbers of players until five on a side was decided to be the right number.

College teams began to play each other, as well as teams from YMCAs and sports clubs.

The first "professional" game probably happened in Trenton, New Jersey, on November 7, 1896. The Trenton YMCA basketball team hosted the Brooklyn YMCA at a local Masonic temple. The teams charged admission. So many people showed up at the game that the teams had money left over after they paid all their expenses. They gave the extra money to the players.

During the next few decades, dozens of professional leagues popped up all around the country. Most disappeared after a year or two.

One of the few that lasted more than a few years was the National Basketball League (NBL). Started in 1935 as the Midwest Basketball Conference, the NBL had businesses sponsor their teams. So the teams had names such as the Akron Goodyear Wingfoots, Chicago American Gears, Fort Wayne General Electrics, and Toledo Jim White Chevrolets.

The NBL had some terrific players, such as centers George Mikan, Leroy "Cowboy" Edwards, and sharpshooting guard Bobby McDermott. But the league played mostly in small cities and arenas.

After World War II ended in 1945, Naismith's game needed a bigger stage. Bigger cities and a bigger, better league.

The National Basketball Association was born. The NBA.

TWO

HARD TIMES

The NBA, known then as the Basketball Association of America (BAA), tipped off on November 1, 1946 when the New York Knicks played the Toronto Huskies at the Maple Leaf Gardens in Toronto. Ossie Schectman of the Knicks scored the first basket and the Knicks won, 68–66. The next season, the Huskies were out of the league and so was Schectman.

The early years of the NBA were not easy. Baseball was the king of professional sports and the NBA struggled to survive.

Franchises came and went. There were eleven teams that first season. The number dipped to eight the next season, then rose to twelve when four National Basketball League (NBL) teams, including the Minneapolis Lakers, joined the league. By the 1949–50 season there were seventeen teams.

Minneapolis dominated the early going, winning five championships from 1949 to 1954. George Mikan, the Lakers big (six feet, ten inches; 245 pounds) center was the NBA's first star. As sportswriter Frank Deford said years later: "Mikan showed that a big man could be a genuine athlete."

Mikan was such a big deal that when the Lakers played the New York Knicks on December 14, 1949 the sign outside Madison Square Garden read:

GEO MIKAN v/s KNICKS

But most of the NBA franchises were barely getting by. In 1950, six teams—the Chicago Stags, St. Louis Bombers, Anderson Packers, Sheboygan Red Skins, Waterloo Hawks, and Denver

Nuggets—folded or left the league. Walter Brown, the owner of the Boston Celtics, had to take a loan out against his house and sell his furniture just to keep his team going.

Teams would do almost anything to get people interested in this new sport of professional basketball. The Celtics had a first round draft choice from Yale, Tony Lavelli. It turned out he wasn't much of a ballplayer, but he was a good musician. So he was paid extra to play the accordion during halftime at their games!

That's right. Lavelli would play the first half, rest a few minutes and then put on his sweats and entertain the crowd with such 1940s hits as "Granada" and "Lady of Spain."

In addition, teams played lots of preseason games to get fans excited about the NBA. In 1959, the Celtics played ten exhibition games against the Minneapolis Lakers in thirteen days in high school gyms in towns all over New England.

Life was not easy for the players during the season either. There were no private team jets as there are for teams today. Players traveled mostly by train. And the trains were not always pulling into big cities such as New York, Boston, or Washington, D.C.

Tom Heinsohn, a high-scoring forward for the Boston Celtics, recalled the early train trips between Rochester, New York and Fort Wayne, Indiana.

"There was no direct way to get there. [The team] would make an arrangement with one of the railroads that you took this train at eleven o'clock at night, and it would get into Indiana and it would pass through cornfields about twenty miles outside of Fort Wayne. They would stop the train, and you would get off in the cornfield and thumb a ride from the high school kids to Fort Wayne."

The players didn't seem to mind. "We were getting paid to play a child's game," Hall of Famer Bob Cousy said years later. "And that was good enough."

Still, most players and coaches needed to work second jobs during the off-season to make ends meet and support their families. Vern Mikkelsen, All-Star forward for the Minneapolis Lakers, was a teacher. Al Bianchi of the Syracuse Nationals worked construction and Gene Shue of the Fort Wayne (later Detroit) Pistons sold insurance. John Havlicek was a manufacturer's representative.

Even the legendary Arnold "Red" Auerbach had a side job as a salesman in the cellophane business in addition to his duties as head coach and general manager of the Boston Celtics. Sometimes, Auerbach would take one of his players along on his sales calls.

Still, some sportswriters did not hide their dislike of the new professional sport and its gigantic players. Shirley Povich, columnist for the *Washington Post*, wrote, "Basketball is for the birds . . . the gooney birds."

As late as 1958, an article appeared in the *Saturday Evening Post*, one of the most popular magazines in the country, titled: "Does Pro Basketball Have a Future?"

But slowly the important elements of the professional game started coming together. . . .

The 24-second clock . . . more and better players . . . and a fast moving, exciting game.

The NBA definitely had a future.

THREE

24 SECONDS

They didn't look like two guys who could save the NBA. Danny Biasone was short, bald, and had never played basketball. He owned a bowling alley in Syracuse, New York, along with the Syracuse Nationals, one of the earliest NBA teams.

Leo Ferris was the Nationals general manager. He was more of a numbers guy than an athlete.

But Biasone and Ferris had been around long enough to know the NBA was in trouble. Big trouble.

In the early 1950s, pro basketball had become little more than a game of keep away and foul shots. One team would grab a lead and then stall, letting the clock run down, and not even trying to make a basket. The other team was forced to foul to get the ball back.

There wasn't enough scoring. Not enough action. And fans were staying away. Eight NBA teams folded in the years between 1950 and 1954.

One game on November 22, 1950, Murray Mendenhall, the head coach of the Fort Wayne Pistons, figured his team didn't stand a chance if they played straight basketball against the powerful Minneapolis Lakers and their superstar center George Mikan. So Mendenhall ordered his point guard Ralph Johnson to stall . . . the whole game.

Mendenhall's strategy worked. The Pistons upset the Lakers 19–18 on a last-second hook shot by Fort Wayne center Larry Foust.

But it wasn't an entertaining game. The two teams scored only eight baskets the entire night. The rest of the points were foul shots. In the fourth quarter the Pistons scored three points and the Lakers scored one. There were long stretches where players were just standing around.

"It wasn't very exciting," Lakers forward Vern Mikkelsen recalled later. "We had a big crowd that night, but a lot of people had walked out."

Later that season the Indianapolis Olympians beat the Rochester Royals by two points in six (!) overtimes. Sounds exciting until you learn that the two teams scored only a few baskets during the six overtimes. Players held on to the ball hoping for a last shot.

In a 1953 playoff game between the Boston Celtics and the Syracuse Nationals there were 106 fouls and 129 foul shots. Keep away and foul shots. Pro basketball was dying.

So as Biasone and Ferris sat in the Eastwood Sports Center sipping coffee with the Syracuse Nationals' head scout, Emil Barboni, in the spring of 1954, they knew they had to do something to speed up the game and keep the action going.

For Biasone, time was the key. There should be a way to force teams to take a shot within a certain amount of time.

Ferris, the numbers guy, took a napkin from the coffee shop and started to jot down some figures. The men looked at the box scores of NBA games they enjoyed. Games in which there was no stalling and the action was nonstop.

They figured the teams in such games took about sixty shots each from the field. That was 120 shots for the game. An NBA game is forty-eight minutes. Sixty seconds in a minute. That's 2,880 seconds.

So . . . 2,880 seconds divided by 120 shots is twenty-four seconds for each shot. What the game needed was a 24-second clock.

On August 10, 1954, Biasone assembled some of the biggest names in basketball, including Red Auerbach, the head coach and general manager of the Boston Celtics and legendary college coach Clair Bee, at Biasone's old high school, Blodgett Vocational. They were there to watch a scrimmage with some Nationals, including All-Star forward Dolph Schayes, and college players.

This game was different because it was played with a 24-second clock. A team had to attempt a shot (and hit the rim) within twenty-four seconds or the other team got the ball.

The basketball bigwigs must have liked what they saw. The NBA used the new 24-second clock in their preseason games that year. The new rule was in place for the NBA's 1954–55 season.

The new rule and clock worked right away. In the previous season (1953–54) NBA teams averaged only 79.5 points a game. With the 24-second clock, the teams averaged 93.1 points a game. And Biasone's Nationals won the NBA title.

The scores kept going up. By the 1957–58 season, every NBA team was averaging more than one hundred points a game.

The fans liked the high-scoring action. Attendance shot up almost 40 percent in the next few years.

Maurice Podoloff, the NBA's first commissioner, said years later, "Whatever the NBA is today is due to one little guy—Danny Biasone. If it hadn't been for him, the NBA would not have lasted."

Biasone may not have looked like someone who would save the NBA, but he did.

FOUR

CLEARING THE LANE

LeBron James, Stephen Curry, James Harden—many of today's greatest players are African American. In fact, almost 75 percent of the NBA players are Black.

But during the first four seasons of the NBA (1946–1949) there were no African American players. Zero.

It wasn't that African Americans were not playing basketball. There were plenty of all-Black teams. City teams such as the Philadelphia Panthers, the Loendi Big Five in Pittsburgh, and the Washington 12 Streeters played in the early years.

Two of the best were the New York Renaissance and the Harlem Globetrotters. The Rens and the Trotters toured the country playing, and beating, all kinds of teams.

The Rens had an eighty-eight-game winning streak in 1933. The Globetrotters usually won so easily they started to add funny bits and ball-handling tricks to keep the crowd entertained. By the late 1940s, the Globetrotters mostly played a brand of comic basketball that fans loved.

But they played straight basketball too. From 1939 to 1948, the best pro teams, White and Black, competed in the World Professional Basketball (WPB) Tournament. The New York Rens, led by William "Pop" Gates, won the first championship in 1939, beating the Oshkosh All-Stars 34–25. The Globetrotters won the title the next year by edging the Chicago Bruins 31–29.

Another all-Black team, the Washington Bears (with Pop Gates, who had switched teams), won the tournament in 1943. The Rens lost in the finals of the last WPB tournament in 1948 to the

Minneapolis Lakers, 75–71. The Lakers went on to win five NBA championships from 1949 to 1954.

So there were plenty of terrific African American basketball players. Still, the NBA was all White in its early years.

America was segregated in the 1940s. African Americans and White people lived in different neighborhoods and went to different schools. Restrictive laws and policies reserved the better schools and neighborhoods for White people. And African Americans were kept from higher-paying jobs.

In the south, White lawmakers required African Americans to sit in the back of buses and to drink from different public water fountains than White people.

Sports were segregated too. Black players were kept out of Major League Baseball for more than sixty years, until 1947, when Jackie Robinson started his career with the Brooklyn Dodgers.

Also, in the early years of the NBA, the comic-style basketball of the Harlem Globetrotters was very popular. The NBA schedule included doubleheaders in which two NBA teams would match up in the first game while the Globetrotters would play a team such as the Washington Generals (who went along with the Globetrotters' antics) in the second, featured game.

The Globetrotters sold lots of tickets at a time when NBA owners were trying to get fans interested in professional basketball. The owners feared if they drafted African American players who would normally play for the Globetrotters this would upset Abe Saperstein, the owner of the Globetrotters. Maybe the Globetrotters would not play in their arenas and the owners would lose money.

Ned Irish, the president of the New York Knicks, finally challenged the unwritten rule against African Americans in 1949 by announcing he wanted to sign Nat "Sweetwater" Clifton of the Globetrotters. The Knicks needed a big man who could rebound and defend. The six-foot, six-inch Clifton filled the bill.

However, the other owners, fearing Saperstein, voted not to allow the Knicks to sign an African American player.

Six months later, Irish came into an NBA Board of Governors meeting and slammed his fist on the table. "Either we get Sweetwater Clifton or we may not stay in the league," he declared.

The New York franchise was important to the NBA. If the league didn't have a team in New York, the league might not survive.

The owners voted six to five to allow teams to draft and sign African American players.

On April 25, 1950, the Boston Celtics drafted Chuck Cooper from Duquesne University in the second round. When someone told Celtics owner Walter Brown that Cooper was Black, Brown replied, "I don't care if he's plaid. All I know is that this kid can play."

In the ninth round, the Washington Capitols chose Earl "Moon Fixer" Lloyd, a six-foot, five-inch leaper out of West Virginia State. Later, the Knicks purchased Sweetwater Clifton's contract from the Globetrotters. The NBA was integrated.

Cooper, Lloyd, and Clifton were never superstars. But these pioneers paved the way for the African American stars to come. Bill Russell arrived in 1956 and dominated the league with his defense and rebounding. Elgin Baylor (1958 to 1972) took the game into the air with his leaping ability. Wilt Chamberlain (1959 to 1973) was simply the most overpowering player in the NBA for years.

Basketball got better when the NBA stopped discriminating and opened up the sport to all players.

SECOND
QUARTER

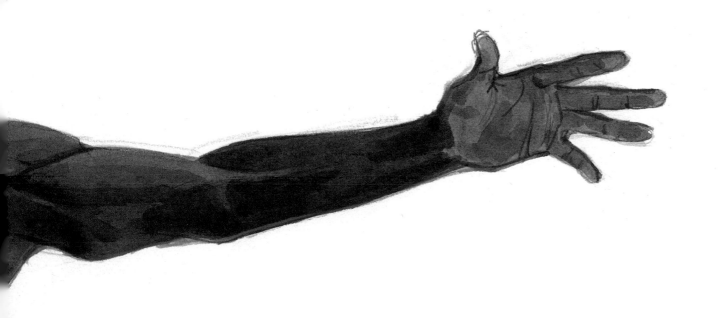

FIVE

THE ICE CAPADES TRADE

In the early 1950s, the Boston Celtics were a good team. But not a great team.

The Celtics had a terrific backcourt. Bob Cousy was a ball-handling wizard who led the NBA in assists. Bill Sharman was a sharpshooting guard who could score from almost anywhere.

But Boston did not have a rugged rebounding center who could get the ball in crucial situations. Instead, the Celtics had "Easy Ed" Macauley. Although Macauley was an All-Star, he was more of a scorer than a rebounder. So every year, the Celtics fell short in the playoffs.

Red Auerbach wanted the Celtics to be great. Auerbach was the team's one-man front office. He was the Celtics head coach and general manager.

Auerbach was also the team's only scout. But he hardly had time to watch college games. He depended on his basketball friends to tell him what players were worth trying to get.

In early 1955, Bill Reinhart, Auerbach's old coach from George Washington University, called him up. Reinhart's team had just returned from the West Coast where they had played the University of San Francisco. Reinhart got right to the point.

"Red, I've seen the guy who can make you into a championship team," he said. "You have to get this guy."

Reinhart was talking about Bill Russell, the University of San Francisco's six-foot, ten-inch center.

How was Russell at offense? Auerbach asked. *Was he a scorer?* Not really, Reinhart answered. But it didn't matter. He could rebound and play defense like nobody else.

So Auerbach started to pay attention to Russell. He had to be impressed. Russell's team won the 1955 and 1956 NCAA Championships losing only one game.

The problem was the Celtics had the seventh pick in the 1956 NBA draft. Even though NBA teams didn't do a lot of scouting, there was no way a player like Russell would last until the seventh pick.

So Auerbach got to work. He knew the Celtics could not keep going with the same players and expect to win a championship. Russell would make the Celtics a different—and hopefully better—team.

First, Auerbach traded two future Hall of Famers, forward Cliff Hagan and center "Easy Ed" Macauley, to the St. Louis Hawks for the Hawks' pick in the 1956 NBA draft.

But this trade only got Boston the second pick in the draft. Auerbach had to do something to make sure the Rochester Royals, the team with the first pick, did not select Russell.

Auerbach had another idea. An idea that would lead to the strangest—and maybe most important—deal in the history of the NBA.

Walter Brown, the owner of the Celtics, was also the president of the Ice Capades, a popular ice-skating show starring several Olympic champions. According to Auerbach, Brown assured the owner of the Rochester Royals that the Ice Capades would appear at the Rochester arena for a series of shows if the Royals did not pick Russell.

It may have been the money the Ice Capades would bring . . . or the money it would have cost for the cash-strapped Royals to sign Russell . . . or the fact that the Royals already had a good young center in Maurice Stokes. Whatever the reason, the Royals selected Sihugo Green, a six-foot, two-inch guard from Duquesne University.

The Celtics had Russell. And Auerbach was delighted . . . until the first time he saw him play.

Russell was playing with the 1956 United States Summer Olympics team in an exhibition at the University of Maryland. Auerbach attended to see his prize draft choice.

Russell was terrible. "I literally felt sick," Auerbach later recalled. "I thought . . . this is the guy I traded Hagan and Macauley for?"

When Russell saw Auerbach he apologized. "I'm sorry," he said. "I was nervous . . . It won't happen again."

Russell was right. The moment he arrived in the NBA he was a superstar. Russell became a five-time Most Valuable Player and twelve-time All-Star. He averaged more than twenty-two rebounds a game

during his career. And Russell was a fearsome defensive player who blocked countless shots and caused players to miss even more.

As Don Nelson observed, "Russell was just such an incredible athlete and didn't care about anything other than winning."

Russell and the Celtics did a lot of winning. Boston won eleven NBA championships in Russell's thirteen seasons (1957–69). The Celtics became the greatest dynasty in the history of professional sports. Year after year, the Celtics beat great teams with fabulous players, such as:

- The Los Angeles Lakers with Jerry West and Elgin Baylor
- The Philadelphia Warriors (and 76ers) with Wilt Chamberlain
- The Cincinnati Royals with Oscar Robertson

All because they drafted Bill Russell . . . with maybe a little help from the Ice Capades.

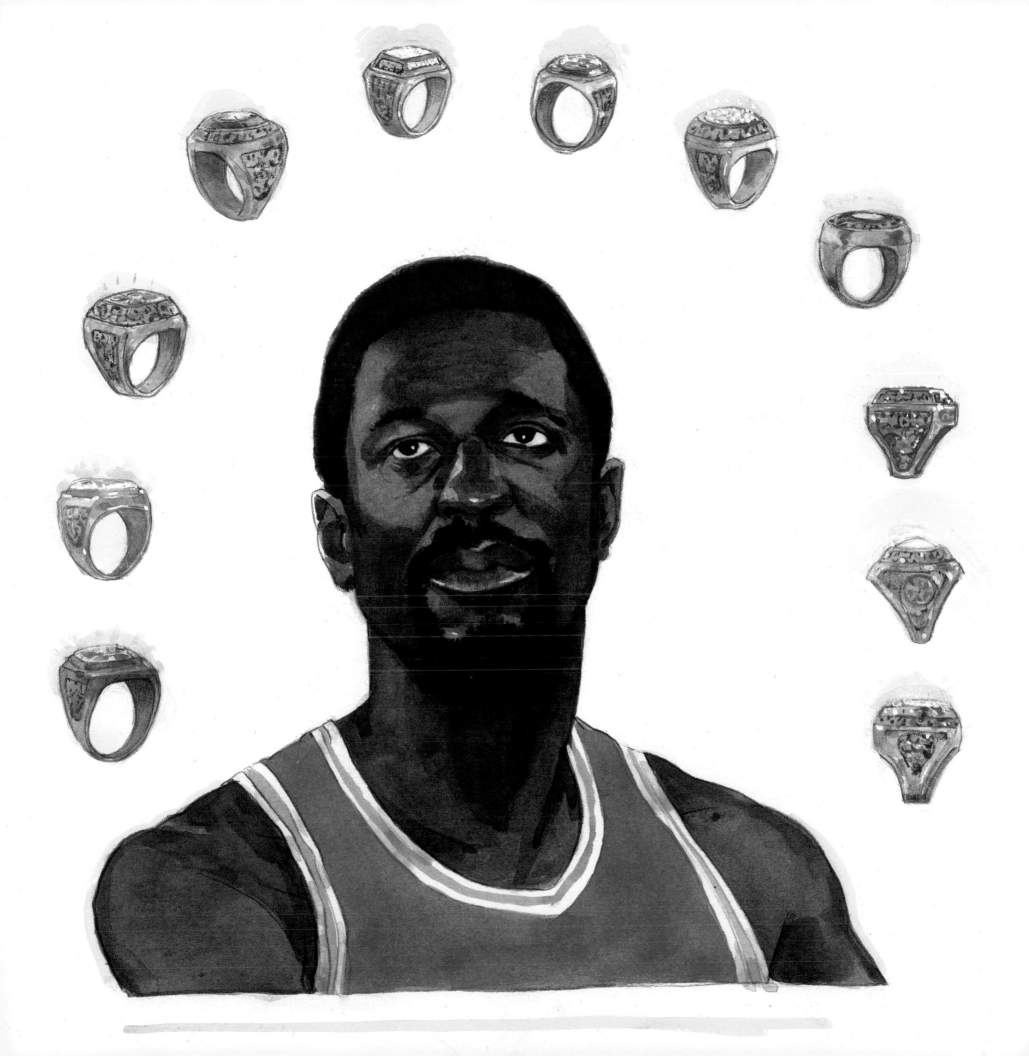

SIX

WILT'S CENTURY MARK

The most amazing achievement in the history of the NBA happened in . . . Hershey, Pennsylvania. In a drafty gym with no television cameras and only two newspaper photographers. One of the photographers left early in the game.

In the early 1960s, NBA teams played some games in smaller cities to get fans interested in pro basketball. The Boston Celtics played in Providence, Rhode Island. The Los Angeles Lakers traveled up the Pacific coast to Portland, Oregon, and Seattle, Washington. And the Philadelphia Warriors played a handful of games in Hershey.

So on March 2, 1962, the Warriors team bus was rolling through the Pennsylvania countryside to play a game against the New York Knicks in a converted ice rink that was home to a minor league hockey team called the Hershey Bears.

One player was not on the bus, preferring to drive to Hershey in his fancy car. Wilt Chamberlain—Wilt the Stilt, the Big Dipper—was not your average NBA player. The seven-foot, one-inch center had been a star since he played at Overbrook High School in West Philadelphia.

Wilt signed with the Warriors in 1959, and promptly rewrote the NBA record books. He led the league in points scored and rebounds in his first two seasons pouring in thirty-eight points a game and snagging more than twenty-seven rebounds.

Wilt wasn't just tall, he was a great athlete. He could dead lift 625 pounds. Wilt could sail twenty-three feet in a running broad jump and once ran a 440-yard race in forty-nine seconds.

Wilt was "the most perfect instrument ever made by God to play basketball," according to Syracuse Nationals star Dolph Schayes.

In 1962, the Big Dipper was having his greatest season. Wilt was averaging more than fifty points a game while grabbing more than twenty-five rebounds.

Bill Russell, the center for the world champion Boston Celtics and Wilt's greatest rival, was impressed. A month before the game in Hershey, Russell observed, "The only way to stop Wilt . . . is to lock him in the dressing room. . . . He has the size, strength, and stamina to score one hundred points some night."

Wilt was on a hot streak when he pulled into the sleepy Pennsylvania town in his white Cadillac convertible. He had scored sixty-seven, sixty-five, and sixty-one points in the Warriors last three games.

Wilt started fast against the Knicks before a crowd of around four thousand fans in a half-empty arena. The big center hit his first five shots on a combination of fadeaway jumpers, spin moves, and Dipper dunks.

By halftime, the Warriors were ahead 79–68, and Wilt had forty-one points. One reason he was piling up points was Wilt had sunk thirteen of his fourteen free throws.

Foul shots were Wilt's one weakness. In his first two seasons in the NBA, Wilt had hit only 58.2 percent and 50.4 percent of his free throws.

Wilt was so desperate, he began to shoot foul shots underhand at the start of the season. Wilt was embarrassed by the underhand shot, but it worked. Wilt was successful on 61.3 percent of his free throws that season.

There may have been another reason for Wilt's great foul shooting that night. The rims at the Hershey Arena were loose. When the circus came to Hershey, the show's clowns used springboards to fly through the air and dunk basketballs and hang on the baskets. The clowns may have loosened the rims.

Whatever the reason, the ball kept going in. By the end of the third quarter, Wilt had sixty-nine points. He was sure to beat his own record of seventy-eight points in an NBA game. And now Wilt's teammates started feeding the big man the ball even more.

The Big Dipper's point total kept going up and up. He got his record-breaking seventy-ninth point on a twenty-foot jump shot. His eighty-ninth point came on a thunderous dunk.

Three more free throws . . . ninety-two points.

A fadeaway jump shot . . . ninety-four points.

A steal. A dish to Wilt . . . ninety-six points.

A fast break and a pass back to Wilt following the play. The big center snapped the ball out of the air and stuffed it into the bucket.

Ninety-eight points. With a minute to go.

Three misses as the seconds ticked away. A Warrior rebound. A high pass inside to Wilt.

The Warriors radio announcer shouted: "He made it! He made it! He made it! A Dipper Dunk!"

One hundred points.

Amazing.

SEVEN

A RED, WHITE, AND BLUE LEAGUE

At the beginning of the 1967–68 season, the NBA had only twelve teams. Of course, pro basketball was not as popular as it is today. Very few NBA games were on television. And when they were, not many people watched. More people watched bowling on TV in the 1960s than basketball.

Still, some folks thought there should be another league. And so the American Basketball Association (ABA) was born.

But the early going was rough. As one of the early ABA team owners, Dick Tinkham, recalled, "Sure, we wanted to merge with the NBA. That was a goal. But a plan? We had none. We went by the seat of our pants and made it up as we went along."

Because it was a new, unknown league, the ABA tried lots of different ways to grab people's attention. ABA teams played a fast-breaking, free-wheeling style, complete with three-point shots. They held the world's first Slam Dunk Contest during an All-Star game.

And of course there was the ball. The ball in the ABA wasn't boring old brown. It was red, white, and blue. Some critics called it a beach ball, but others thought it looked great spinning through the air and into the basket.

And kids loved the flashy ball. They bought millions of red, white, and blue balls through the years.

The ABA started with eleven teams in 1967, and ended with seven in 1976. The league lasted nine seasons before four teams—the Denver Nuggets, Indiana Pacers, New York Nets, and San Antonio Spurs—merged with the NBA.

During those years, the ABA went through more than twenty-five different teams, from the Anaheim Amigos to the Virginia Squires. Some teams, such as the Indiana Pacers, Kentucky Colonels, and Denver Rockets/Nuggets, played all nine seasons while others, such as the Baltimore Claws, lasted only three exhibition games.

The league also went through millions of dollars as the teams battled the more established NBA for star players. The ABA signed such NBA stars as Rick Barry and Billy Cunningham as well as numerous college players to big-money contracts. The ABA even signed several NBA . . . referees!

But the ABA always had interesting players. At first, some were more interesting as personalities than as basketball players. Characters such as Maurice "Toothpick" McHartley, a six-foot, three-inch guard who couldn't play unless he had a toothpick in the corner of his mouth. (DO NOT TRY THIS!)

Les Selvage of the Anaheim Amigos chucked up an unbelievable 461 three-point shots during his first—and only—full season in the ABA.

Then there was Charlie "Helicopter" Hentz. This six-foot, five-inch leaper once broke two (!) backboards in a single game with his powerful dunks.

Other ABA players became secret stars. They were every bit as good as anyone in the NBA, but remained unknown because ABA games were almost never televised.

Roger Brown was a six-foot, five-inch scoring machine for the Indiana Pacers who really lit it up during the playoffs. Brown scored fifty-three, thirty-nine, and forty-five points in the last three games in a series against the Los Angeles Stars to clinch the 1970 ABA title.

"Little Louie" Dampier was a six-foot guard who could score from anywhere, but especially from in back of the three-point line. Dampier appeared in seven ABA All-Star games during his nine-year career with the Kentucky Colonels.

Other ABA players became Hall of Fame, household names after the merger. Julius Erving, also known as "Dr. J.," became a hoops legend for his high-flying, windmilling dunks during his five-year ABA career.

As Steve Jones, who played eight seasons in the ABA, said, "I guarded Julius [when he was in the ABA]; it wasn't much fun. . . . The only other player in the same class is Michael Jordan . . . and [Julius] was a far better rebounder than Michael."

George "the Iceman" Gervin was a rail-thin (six feet, seven inches; 180 pounds) player who could score on an endless variety of jump shots, fade-aways, and finger rolls. Gervin kept scoring when his San Antonio Spurs joined the NBA. Gervin led the NBA in scoring for four seasons.

In the first year after the ABA merged with the NBA, ten of the twenty-four players named to the 1977 NBA All-Star Game were former ABA players.

The ABA stars were not a secret anymore. They were stars in the NBA.

EIGHT

A LINE ON THE FLOOR

I t's just a line. An arc on the floor drawn twenty-three feet, nine inches from the basket at either end of the court.

But that line has changed the game of basketball and the NBA.

Past that line, a basket now counts for three points. In front of the line, a basket counts for just two. So, long-range sharpshooters such as Stephen Curry, James Harden, and Klay Thompson shoot hundreds of three-pointers every season.

The three-point basket was not always part of the NBA and the game of basketball. In the earliest games a basket, any basket, was one point. Quickly, however, a basket made from anywhere on the floor became two points while a foul shot was one point. This scoring arrangement stayed that way for a long time, although there were some people pushing for change.

Howard Hobson was a terrific basketball coach. He led the University of Oregon to the first NCAA men's basketball championship defeating Ohio State 46–33 in 1939.

Hobson was also an early advocate of the three-point basket. He thought it would add excitement to the game. He left Oregon to go to graduate school at Columbia University in New York City and brought the idea of a three-point basket with him.

On February 7, 1945, Hobson arranged for two New York City colleges, Fordham and Columbia, to play an experimental game with a three-point line drawn twenty-one feet from the basket.

Columbia beat Fordham 73–58. The teams made twenty three-point shots between them. The fans

and players liked the three-point basket. But some sports-writers who were at the game, as well as several important basketball people, did not like the new rule. They saw no reason to change.

In 1961, Abe Saperstein, the owner of the Harlem Globetrotters, started an eight-team league called the American Basketball League (ABL) to challenge the more established NBA. The league only lasted for one season (1961–62) and part of another.

The ABL experimented with the three-point shot. But the league folded so quickly basketball fans hardly noticed.

The American Basketball Association (ABA) came along a few years later in 1967. The ABA tried lots of things to get the attention of fans. The red, white, and blue ball. A wide-open, high scoring style of play. And a three-point shot.

During the early years of the ABA, some players, such as "Little Louie" Dampier, Chico Vaughn, and Glen "the Kentucky Rifle" Combs, became experts at firing up and making three-pointers. The simple arithmetic of "three for two" made it a good shot.

When the NBA merged with the ABA by taking on four ABA teams in 1976, the older league did not take on the three-point shot right away. The NBA finally adopted the three-pointer during the 1979–80 season.

While some individual players embraced the new long shot, many NBA teams continued to work the ball in closer to the basket for "better" shots. For example, in the 1980 NBA Finals the Los Angeles Lakers, led by Kareem Abdul-Jabbar and Earvin "Magic" Johnson, defeated the Philadelphia 76ers and Julius Erving in a six-game series.

The Lakers did not make a single three-point shot during the series and only attempted four long shots. The Sixers were not tossing them up either. Philadelphia made one three-pointer out of sixteen attempts.

Gradually, the three-point shot became a bigger part of the NBA game. Great shooters such as Peja Stojaković, Ray Allen, and Reggie Miller began to specialize in the long bomb.

As five-time NBA championship head coach Gregg Popovich of the San Antonio Spurs observed, "[The three-point shot] is a heck of a weapon. . . . To me it's not basketball, but you've got to use it. If you don't, you're in big trouble."

Now, the three-point shot is a huge part of the NBA game. James Harden took 1,028 three-point shots during the 2018–19 regular season. That is more than twelve long bombs a game—an unthinkable number even to the most shot-happy ABA player.

But Harden should keep taking them. After all, he made 378 of the long shots. That's almost five extra points every game for his team.

It's not just Harden who is taking the shots. Today, even big men and centers such as Kristaps Porziņģis, Joel Embiid, and Karl-Anthony Towns will step out and put up a three-pointer.

In the 2021 NBA playoffs, several teams, including the champion Milwaukee Bucks, attempted thirty-five or more three-point shots a game.

These days, the three-point shot is as common as a layup or midrange jumper.

Howard Hobson would be proud.

The Knicks were New York's NBA team from the very beginning. But in the early days they didn't have much of a team. Their owner, Ned Irish, wouldn't even let the Knicks play in his building, Madison Square Garden, for lots of their games. Irish stuck the pros in the 69th Regiment Armory, a cavernous building in Manhattan, and staged doubleheaders of the more popular local college teams such as St. Johns, Long Island University, and New York University at the Garden.

The Knicks finished first in the Eastern Division during the 1953–1954 season, but were bounced quickly from the playoffs. By the 1960s, the Knicks were at the bottom of the NBA, suffering through eight straight losing seasons (from 1959–60 to 1966–67).

But on December 19, 1968, the Knicks traded Walt Bellamy and Howie Komives for rugged forward Dave DeBusschere of the Detroit Pistons and things started to

happen. The Knicks won three quarters of their games for the remainder of the season. They took the Boston Celtics to a hard-fought sixth game before losing the Division Finals to the reigning world champions.

With Bill Russell retiring from the Celtics, the Knicks felt that next season would be their year. They were right.

The Knicks got off to a great start in the fall of 1969, racking up a record of 23–1 in the first two months, and coasted through the rest of the season.

New York had an unlikely group of personalities who blended together perfectly. They followed the instructions of their head coach, Red Holzman, who had played ball at Franklin K. Lane High School in Brooklyn and at City College: to see the ball; pass to an open teammate; and on defense, "deny, deny, deny."

The Knicks needed all their teamwork in the 1970s playoffs. Especially

eight minutes into the crucial fifth game of the Finals, when they were ten points down to the Los Angeles Lakers, and New York's captain and center, Willis Reed, went down with a painful leg injury.

But the Knicks came back with the sharpshooting of forwards Bill Bradley and Cazzie Russell, and the cool leadership of Walt Frazier to win that fifth game 107–100.

The Knicks won it all in Game 7, 113–99, when Reed limped onto the floor of a packed Madison Square Garden, hit the first two baskets of the game, and gave his team twenty-seven minutes of hard-nosed defense against the Lakers' Wilt Chamberlain.

Of course, Walt Frazier's thirty-six points and nineteen assists helped a bit too.

The Knicks were the champions of the NBA. They had done it in the Big Apple with all its television networks, newspapers, and publishing houses. Everyone wanted a piece of the Knicks. They won it all again in 1973. There were books, a million newspaper and magazine articles, and even a new and better television contract for the NBA in the years to come.

At last, the Knicks and the NBA were the toast of New York City. The greatest basketball players on the best team in biggest basketball town of them all.

TEN

BIRD AND MAGIC

In some ways, they were very different from each other.

One was White and from rural Indiana, the little town of French Lick. A quiet kid who walked away from a basketball scholarship at Indiana University and went to work for his hometown, cutting trees, sweeping the streets, and collecting garbage. After a year of making money, he enrolled at Indiana State University.

The other was Black, a city kid from Lansing, Michigan, who carried a cool nickname from the time he was fifteen and had a smile that could light up any room. His decision to play basketball at Michigan State instead of the University of Michigan was front-page news.

But in other ways—the most important ways—they were exactly alike.

Both were big men—six-feet, nine-inches tall—who could really pass and handle the ball. Neither player was known for his speed or his high-flying dunks, but they had a knack for making everyone around them better.

Most of all, they were cold-blooded competitors who would do anything to win.

Larry Bird and "Magic" Johnson entered the NBA in 1979 as the most highly anticipated rookies in years. Earlier that spring the two had squared off in the NCAA Finals. Magic's Michigan State Spartans had beaten Bird and his Indiana State teammates 75–64, in what is still the highest rated college basketball game in television history.

Bird and Magic promptly turned their teams—and the entire NBA—around.

Bird took a Boston Celtics team that had won just twenty-nine games the year before and led them to the playoffs with a regular season record of 61–21. He won the Rookie of the Year Award going away.

In the playoffs, the Celtics lost to the Philadelphia 76ers, who went on to battle the Los Angeles Lakers and their rookie sensation, Magic Johnson, in the NBA Finals.

How did Magic do? He played one of the most amazing games in basketball history to clinch the championship for the Lakers.

The Lakers were leading the Philadelphia 76ers with three games to two in a best-of-seven series. But Kareem Abdul-Jabbar, the Lakers' center and the greatest scorer in NBA history, was sidelined during the fifth game with an ankle injury.

With Abdul-Jabbar on crutches, Coach Paul Westhead put Magic in the pivot. The rookie responded with forty-two points, fifteen rebounds, and seven assists to lead the Lakers to a 123–107 win and the title.

Magic and Bird kept winning throughout the 1980s. In fact, either the Lakers or the Celtics (or both) appeared in every one of the NBA Finals from 1980 to 1989, with the Lakers winning five titles and the Celtics winning three.

It wasn't just that Magic and Bird won so many championships, it was the way they played the game that captivated basketball fans all around the world. Magic's and Bird's eyes were always searching the court. They passed the ball and got everyone involved. Magic and Bird made NBA basketball a team game again.

As Kevin McHale, a Hall of Fame forward on Bird's Celtics teams, once observed: "Larry and Magic are still the only two guys I know who could take ten or eleven shots and still dominate the game."

Kurt Rambis, one of Magic's Lakers teammates, agreed. "They didn't need to do it themselves. They were happy to make the pass."

And they played flat out from start to finish. As long-time NBA coach and executive Donnie Walsh said, "Larry and Magic played hard from the first possession to the last. They didn't take a single play off, and they forced their teammates to match their intensity."

Bird and Magic were always working on their game. Adding a wrinkle or two over the summer months to make them more dangerous during the season.

After a disappointing 1982–83 season in which the Celtics did not make it to the Finals, Bird decided he needed to add a step-back jump shot to his arsenal of offensive moves. So that summer he shot eight hundred (!) step-back jumpers a day at his home in Indiana.

Magic was not a great shooter when he came into the league. But he practiced and got better, especially from the free throw line. Magic led the NBA in free throw shooting during the 1988–89 season, hitting 91.1 percent of his foul shots.

And the rest of the NBA, they came along for the ride. The popularity of pro basketball soared during the 1980s with Bird and Magic. The 1980 NBA Finals—the one that Magic won with forty-two points in the sixth and final game—could only be seen late at night on tape delay. That's right, none of the television networks would put it on live.

As one NBA official later recalled, "We were regarded as being somewhere between mud wrestling and tractor pulling."

By the end of the 1980s, everything was different because of Bird and Magic.

The NBA was in prime time.

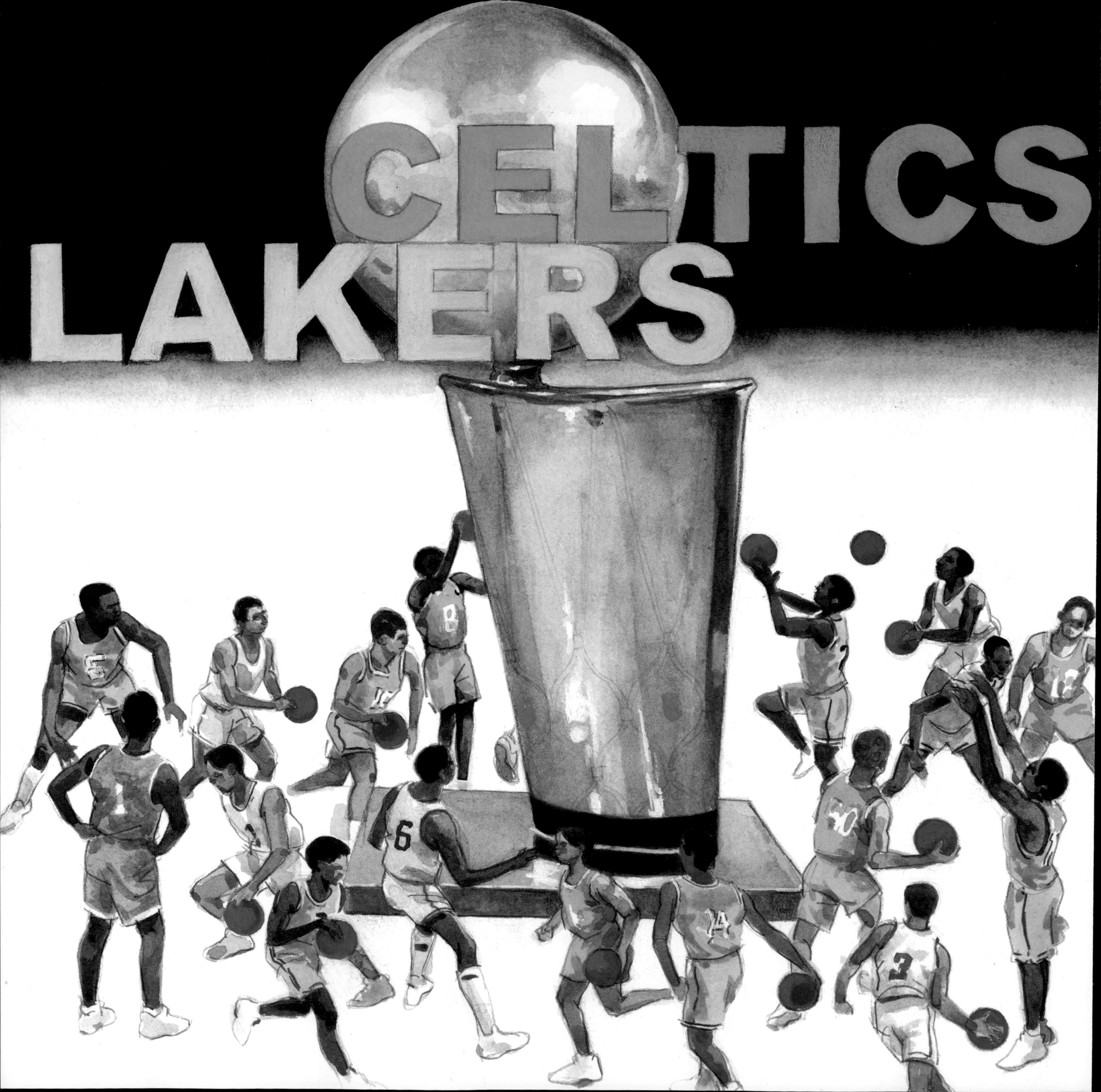
CELTICS
LAKERS

ELEVEN

THE BEST OF RIVALS

I t wasn't just Bird and Magic. The rivalry between the Celtics and the Lakers started long before either of them showed up.

Two teams. One East Coast, the other West Coast. Two teams eyeing each other, measuring themselves against the other. The biggest rivalry in the NBA.

The Lakers started in Minnesota—the land of ten thousand lakes—as the Minneapolis Lakers. They dominated the early years of the NBA with a big frontline of George Mikan, Vern Mikkelsen, and Jim "The Kangaroo Kid" Pollard. Minneapolis won five NBA titles from 1949 to 1954.

The Celtics took off when they drafted center Bill Russell in 1956, and started winning championships with a high-scoring, fast-breaking style of play. Boston trounced Minneapolis in four straight games to win their second NBA championship in 1959.

The Lakers moved west to Los Angeles in 1960. But more importantly they drafted a skinny shooting guard from West Virginia University named Jerry West.

West was an instant star. He teamed with forward Elgin Baylor to give Los Angeles a dynamic duo— Mr. Inside (Baylor) and Mr. Outside (West)—that would challenge the Celtics throughout the 1960s.

Baylor was a powerful forward whose ability to stay airborne while shooting gave the phrase "hang time" to the game of basketball. As one writer said, "[Baylor] never broke the law of gravity, but he [was] awfully slow in obeying it."

Baylor and West challenged Boston, but never beat them for a championship. The Celtics met the

57

Lakers in the NBA Finals six times from 1962 to 1969, and the Celtics walked away with the title every time. As Laker power forward Rudy LaRusso observed years later, "We had a star system; they had a great team."

The Lakers came close. In the seventh and final game of the 1962 Finals, the Lakers had the ball with the score tied 100–100, and 13,909 Boston fans screaming at the top of their lungs in the Boston Garden. Time out with five seconds to go.

The Lakers tried to get the ball to West or Baylor, but the Celtics had the two Lakers stars covered. Instead, "Hot Rod" Hundley slipped a pass to Frank Selvy for a wide-open ten-foot baseline jumper. The ball bounced high off the back rim, and Bill Russell grabbed the rebound.

Russell, who scored thirty points and grabbed forty rebounds, would not let the Celtics lose in overtime. The Celtics won 110–107.

From 1980 through 1986, the Celtics and Lakers traded the NBA championship back and forth, with the Celtics winning in '81, '84 and '86, and the Lakers winning in '80, '82 and '85. Three titles apiece.

Boston and Los Angeles had great teams. The Celtics had Bird and they also had a frontline that included Kevin McHale and Robert Parish. They needed every big man they could get, because Los Angeles had Kareem Abdul-Jabbar, perhaps the most unstoppable scorer in the history of the game with his "sky hook."

The two teams were matched up again in 1987, in a series the whole basketball world had been waiting for. The Lakers won the first two games in L.A. but the Celtics came back to win Game 3 in the Garden.

Game 4 was a back-and-forth classic. The Lakers grabbed the lead, 107–106, when Magic tossed in what was called a "junior sky hook" high over the outstretched arms of Kevin McHale and Robert Parish with two seconds left.

Time out! The Celtics had a chance for one more shot.

Dennis Johnson tossed the ball in the corner to the suddenly wide-open Larry Bird—the man who had won so many games on so many last-second shots they called him "Larry Legend."

"That ball is straight—it is straight as an arrow," Lakers head coach Pat Riley recalled thinking years later. "That's going in."

That ball bounced off the back of the rim, just as it had twenty-five years before for Frank Selvy. So close, but not close enough. The Lakers were on their way, winning in '87 and in '88, and staking their claim as the greatest team of the 1980s.

Michael Jordan and the Chicago Bulls dominated the 1990s, but the Lakers won six more titles in the 2000s with such standout players as Kobe Bryant, Shaquille "Shaq" O'Neal, and LeBron James. One of the championships came when they beat the Celtics in a seven-game Finals series in 2010.

That was payback for the 2008 Finals when the Celtics, led by Kevin Garnett, Paul Pierce, and Ray Allen, had beaten the Lakers in six games.

It's always been the Celtics and the Lakers. East Coast, West Coast. Seventeen championships for the Celtics. Seventeen championships for the Lakers. Two teams and the greatest rivalry in the NBA.

TWELVE

AIR JORDAN

One player who tried his hardest to break the Lakers and Celtics stranglehold on the NBA championship was Michael Jordan.

Picked third in the 1984 draft by the Chicago Bulls, Jordan was a star right away. He was voted Rookie of the Year during his first season. In his third season, Jordan won his first of a record ten scoring titles, averaging an incredible 37.1 points per game.

But success in the playoffs? For years, Jordan was a slam-dunk All-Star, but not an NBA champion. Jordan had his moments, such as the 1986 game in the first round of the playoffs against the Celtics in Boston Garden, when he scored sixty-three points. Still, the Celtics beat the Bulls 135–131 in double overtime and drummed the Bulls out of the playoffs.

Jordan was disappointed. When asked about his sixty-three-point performance, he said, "I'd give all the points back if we could have won the game."

The Bulls slowly started to get better when forwards Scottie Pippen and Horace Grant joined the team in 1987. More wins came as the years passed.

Jordan kept getting better too. Never satisfied with being one of the NBA's biggest stars, he kept adding new moves, new skills to his game.

Following his first pro season, Jordan returned to his alma mater, the University of North Carolina, and asked then assistant coach Roy Williams what he needed to do to become better. Williams said if Jordan improved his jump shot he would be unstoppable. So that summer and for many summers after

that, Jordan worked on his jump shot, taking countless shots in empty gyms.

Long before he won his first NBA championship, Jordan was a winner with advertisers. Handsome and charming, with an almost otherworldly basketball talent, Jordan endorsed such iconic American brands as McDonalds, Coca-Cola, and Gatorade.

Nike took a chance with the young rookie superstar in 1984. Until then, the sports brand paid lots of players to wear Nike shoes. Changing course, Nike decided to direct all its endorsement money and energy into one player . . . Jordan. Nike even gave him his own line of shoes . . . Air Jordans.

Air Jordans took off, aided by a series of irresistible television ads by director Spike Lee, and the tagline: "It's gotta be the shoes." Sales of the shoes have never slowed down. In 2019, years after Jordan had hung up his basketball shoes, it was estimated that Nike made $3.14 billion from the Jordan brand in twelve months, and that Jordan earned around $130 million from his Nike connection.

Jordan, however, suffered several more seasons of playoff frustration. The Bulls lost to the Detroit Pistons three years in a row, from 1988 to 1990. Following the loss of the seventh game of the 1990 Eastern Conference Finals series, Jordan wept in the back of the team bus and wondered whether he and the Bulls would ever break through.

Jordan was the kind of person, the kind of player, who had to win. Years later, Harvest Leroy Smith, a friend who played basketball with Jordan growing up in Wilmington, North Carolina, recalled: "[H]e always had to win. If it was a game of H-O-R-S-E and you beat him, you would have to play another game until he won. You didn't go home until he had won."

In his seventh season in the NBA, Jordan and the Bulls finally won it all. They swept the Pistons in the Eastern Conference Finals 4–0 (four games to none). Then beat the Lakers and Magic Johnson 4–1.

Fueled by Jordan's ferocious competitive drive, the Bulls kept winning. In 1992, they beat the Portland Trailblazers and their star Clyde "the Glide" Drexler. Before the series some had suggested that Drexler, a future Hall of Famer, was as good as Jordan. His Airness silenced such talk by dominating the series, scoring more than thirty-five points a game and hounding Drexler on defense.

The next year, the Bulls beat the Phoenix Suns and Charles Barkley. By then Jordan seemed to have had enough of winning. Saddened by his father's murder, Jordan retired and played minor league baseball. His father had loved baseball.

Baseball, however, was one thing Jordan could not beat. After an unsuccessful season with the Birmingham Barons, Jordan returned to the Bulls and the NBA. And to winning.

Jordan and the Bulls racked up three more championships. Jordan was the Most Valuable Player in each of the three Finals. He retired from the Bulls in 1998, but after three years returned for two non-championship seasons with the Washington Wizards. Jordan retired for good after that, widely recognized as the greatest player in NBA history.

And basketball's greatest salesman.

THIRTEEN

THE DREAM TEAM

Basketball fans argue about what team is the greatest of all time.

Some mention the Golden State Warriors with Stephen Curry. Others claim the Chicago Bulls teams with Michael Jordan, which won six NBA titles, is the best.

Or maybe one of the Magic Johnson "Showtime" Lakers teams of the 1980s. The 1985–86 Boston Celtics team with Larry Bird has its fans too.

Older fans might argue for one of Bill Russell's Celtics teams of the 1960s, or Wilt's powerhouse 1966–67 Philadelphia 76ers.

But the answer is . . . none of the above.

The greatest basketball team of all time was the Dream Team—the 1992 United States Summer Olympics team. And it's not even close.

The Dream Team had Michael Jordan, Magic Johnson, Larry Bird, Charles Barkley, and much more. Eleven of them are Hall of Famers. During their storied NBA careers, the twelve players on the Dream Team won twenty-three NBA championship rings, were named the league's Most Valuable Player fifteen times, and appeared in an incredible 117 All-Star Games.

From 1936, when basketball was introduced as an official Olympic sport, American teams dominated even though the United States only sent its best college players. In 1988, however, America's college players lost in the semifinals to the Russians and only took home the bronze medal.

Shortly after that, the rules were changed and the United States was allowed to send professional

players. So the United States decided to recruit its pro stars to compete in the 1992 Summer Games.

At first, many basketball officials doubted NBA stars would give up their summer vacations to play.

Boy, were they wrong. Magic Johnson said yes quickly, then Michael Jordan got on board. The enthusiasm for the Olympic team was so great that on September 21, 1991, TV announcer Bob Costas hosted a selection show in which he announced ten of the twelve players with all the drama of the Academy Awards.

Magic Johnson . . . Charles Barkley . . . Karl Malone . . . John Stockton . . . Patrick Ewing . . . David Robinson . . . Larry Bird . . . Chris Mullin . . . Scottie Pippen, and . . . Michael Jordan.

The USA Basketball committee named Clyde "the Glide" Drexler and the only college member of the team, NCAA Player of the Year, Christian Laettner, later.

The U.S. team was unstoppable. They raced through six games in the Olympic qualifying tournament, beating teams such as Panama, Cuba, and Venezuela by margins of up to sixty points.

By the time they reached the Olympics in Barcelona, Spain, the Dream Team players were international superstars. Opposing players asked the Dream Teamers for their autographs and posed for pictures *before* the games. Thousands waited outside the Dream Team's hotel just to get a glimpse of the players.

Before the first Olympic game against the African country of Angola, Charles Barkley said, "I don't know nothing 'bout Angola. But Angola's in trouble."

The Dream Team won 116–48.

The Dream Team rolled through the rest of the Olympic competition, winning all their games by at least thirty-two points. Head coach Chuck Daly never called a timeout during the Olympics.

The Dream Team was so good that they had to find competition among themselves. Some of the players played golf, H-O-R-S-E (a basketball shooting game), or Ping-Pong.

Then there was the unforgettable day in Monaco when they were training before the Olympics, when Daly split the squad into two five-man teams led by Magic Johnson and Michael Jordan. The greatest team of all time played each other in an almost empty gym in Monte Carlo. Trash talking the whole time. Playing for nothing but bragging rights

Magic's team jumped off to a quick 7–0 lead. Scottie Pippen finally put Michael's team on the board with a jump shot.

The teams traded baskets as Magic's team clung to a 20–13 lead. Then Jordan powered a layup through four players. 20–15. Pippen made a couple of free throws. 20–17. A Jordan jumper and a thunderous Pippen dunk and Michael's team was leading 21–20.

The game heated up, with all the stars playing hard and arguing calls. With a little more than a minute to play, Michael's team was leading 38–32. A twisting Laettner layup and two Robinson free throws cut the lead to two . . . 38–36.

Time was running down. Jordan spun left and was fouled by Laettner. Two shots. Magic tried to rattle Michael with a few choice words. Jordan drained both free throws. Michael's team won, 40–36.

Years later, Jordan called the Monte Carlo game "the most fun I ever had on a basketball court."

The Dream Team made basketball better because they inspired players all over the world. As NBA official Kim Bohuny said, ". . . I can't begin to tell you how many [international players] say they started watching basketball at the '92 Olympics."

A world of great basketball. Brought to you by the Dream Team.

FOURTEEN

THE GLOBAL GAME

For its first three seasons, the NBA was called the Basketball Association of America (BAA). The name fit. After all, basketball was an American game in the 1940s. Invented in America. Played in America.

While almost every player in the old BAA was an American there were a handful who had been born elsewhere. For the next several decades, the NBA was almost exclusively an American league. But even though the NBA was not bringing in players from abroad, America and the NBA were taking its players and basketball to other countries.

In 1936, amateur basketball players went to Germany to play in the Summer Olympics, the first year basketball was a medal sport. The United States team won the first gold medal, beating Canada 19–8 in a game played outdoors and in the rain! James Naismith, who invented the game, attended the first Olympic basketball games.

But because of World War II (1939–1945), the game was not played again until the 1948 Olympic games in London. The United States continued to dominate most Olympic basketball tournaments. In 1960, for example, the American team was loaded with such future NBA stars and Hall of Famers as Oscar Robertson, Jerry West, Walt Bellamy, and Jerry Lucas. The U.S. team stormed through the tournament, winning their games by an average of forty-one points a game.

As the years went by, however, the international teams and players kept getting better. The best international players wanted to test themselves against the best and play in the NBA.

These international players had to deal with many challenges off the court when they came to the United States to play. Different food. Different culture. And in many cases, a different language.

As Šarūnas Marčiulionis said after he came from Lithuania to play for the Golden State Warriors in the 1990s, he was quiet for most of his first two years in the United States. He said he could understand a lot more English than he could speak.

For some, there was a difference in weather. Hakeem Olajuwon came from tropical Nigeria to look at three colleges, one in New York City, one in North Carolina, and another in Houston, Texas. When Olajuwon stepped out of the airport in New York City in just a shirt and pants, he was hit by a cold wind.

"I ran back inside," Olajuwon recalled. "I had never experienced that kind of cold before."

Olajuwon wanted to get out of New York fast, so he changed his plans and flew to Houston, where the weather was "perfect." He starred for the University of Houston Cougars, leading them to the NCAA finals two consecutive years. Then Olajuwon led the Houston Rockets to two NBA titles in 1994 and 1995.

Olajuwon had great footwork for a seven footer, leaving defenders in the air after multiple fakes. The reason for the fabulous footwork? Olajuwon had played soccer in Nigeria before switching to basketball.

After the sensation of the Dream Team at the 1992 Summer Olympics, more international players came to America to play in college and the NBA. The list is long and impressive and includes such superstars as:

Dirk Nowitzki (fourteen-time All-Star)	Germany
Steve Nash (eight-time All-Star)	Canada
Toni Kukoč (three-time NBA champion)	Croatia
Manu Ginóbili (four-time NBA champion)	Argentina
Yao Ming (Hall of Fame 2016)	China

Now, almost a quarter of the NBA players are from countries other than the United States. At the beginning of the 2020–21 NBA season, 107 international players from forty-one countries were on NBA rosters. Included among the non-American players are some of the biggest stars in the game: Giannis "the Greek Freak" Antetokounmpo (Greece), Joel Embiid (Cameroon), Nikola Jokić (Serbia), Luka Dončić (Slovenia), and Ben Simmons (Australia).

In the future, the game will only become more international. As Hall of Fame coach Pat Riley once observed: "There's a lot of world. There's only 350 million people in America. There's seven billion people around the world. That's a lot of basketball players somewhere. They just need to be found."

FIFTEEN

HIGH SCHOOL TO PRO

They would make quite a team.

Start with Moses Malone, one of the greatest rebounders and scorers in NBA history, at center. Then put all six feet, eleven inches of Kevin Garnett at power forward.

LeBron James has the all-around skills for small forward. As any hoops fan knows, you have to find a place for maybe the greatest player of all time.

Kobe Bryant and Tracy McGrady would make an unstoppable, high-scoring backcourt. Although I don't think this team would have any trouble putting the ball in the basket.

The bench? Three-time Defensive Player of the Year and eight-time All-Star, Dwight Howard, could back up at center. Jermaine O'Neal, Al Harrington, Rashard Lewis, and Amar'e Stoudemire would bring size, scoring, and toughness to the frontcourt.

You have plenty of choices for substitutes in the backcourt depending on what the team needs. J.R. Smith can shoot the three-ball. Shaun Livingston is a pass-first, shoot-second guard. And if you need someone to lock down a high scorer, DeShawn Stevenson is your man. After all, they call him "The Locksmith."

As I said, quite a team. Hard to think of any team other than the Dream Team that could beat this group.

So who is this make-believe team? They are players who entered the NBA straight from high school. Prep to pros.

For most of the history of the NBA, players could not come into the league straight out of high school (although a seven-foot center named Reggie Harding joined the NBA in the early 1960s without attending college). In the 1970s, however, the competition between the rival NBA and ABA for players had become so fierce that the pros were eyeing Moses Malone. Dozens of colleges wanted the high school student from Petersburg, Virginia, but so did the Utah Stars of the ABA.

Malone signed with the Stars. The six-foot, ten-inch center was ready for the rough and tumble of pro ball. Growing up, Malone had played pickup basketball with the convicts at the nearby prison.

Malone was an ABA All-Star his first season. Over the course of his twenty-one-year professional career— two seasons in the ABA and nineteen in the NBA—he grabbed more rebounds than anyone other than Wilt Chamberlain and Bill Russell.

A year later, two more players out of high school— Darryl Dawkins and Bill Willoughby—signed with NBA teams. Neither player lived up to his early potential. Although if there were a Hall of Fame for basketball nicknames, Dawkins, who was sometimes called "Dr. Dunk," "Sir Slam," and "Zandokan the Mad Dunker," would be in it.

It was almost twenty years before an NBA team took a chance on another player right out of high school. In the 1995 draft, the Minnesota Timberwolves took Kevin Garnett from Farragut Career Academy as the fifth overall pick.

The Timberwolves got someone who, according to Minnesota assistant coach Jerry Sichting, was "born to play." Garnett didn't care about late-night partying or

buying fancy clothes. He just wanted to play hoops. Garnett wore a lucky two-dollar bill in his basketball shoes and let the checks from his $5.4 million three-year rookie contract pile up in his locker. Garnett's focus paid off. "KG" was an All-Star in his second year.

More young players followed. In the next two years, NBA teams drafted Kobe Bryant, Tracy McGrady, and Jermaine O'Neal out of high school.

The success of these players and others had NBA scouts visiting high school gyms all over the country. In the 2003 draft, the Cleveland Cavaliers drafted LeBron James as the number one overall pick.

James had been a national sensation as a teenager. Keith Dambrot, his high school coach, said, "Three games into his sophomore year, I knew he would never go to college."

Four other high school players were drafted in 2003. In 2004, NBA teams selected eight more high schoolers. In 2005, nine more.

Not every high school pick turned out to be LeBron James. Korleone Young played all of fifteen minutes in the NBA. James Lang, chosen in the same draft as James, played only eleven games. Ricky Sánchez, drafted in 2005, never played a minute in the NBA.

Thirty of the approximately forty players drafted directly from high school, however, played in the NBA for ten or more seasons.

In June 2005, the NBA made a rule that to be drafted a player had to be nineteen years old and at least one year removed from his high school graduation date. At the same time, the NBA started the NBA Development League—now called the G League—for players who needed more experience or were not quite ready for the big league.

The days of going from high school to the pros were over.

Still, these "prep to pros" would have made quite a team.

SIXTEEN

THE SHOOTERS

*G*reen *grabs the rebound. There's a quick outlet pass to Curry. Curry dribbles up the right side, crosses over, pulls up at the top of the key. Shoots. It's good.*

These days they keep track of almost everything that happens in an NBA game. Offensive rebounds, defensive rebounds, assists, turnovers, steals, blocked shots. But the only action that changes the score is the ball flying through the net. Two pointers, three pointers, and free throws.

In the first few years of the NBA, players on offense would keep passing the ball until they spotted someone with a wide-open shot. The player would plant his feet firmly on the floor and push the ball up from his chest with both hands. A two-hand set shot. It looked funny, but some players were sure shots with the two-hander.

Or if they were lucky, teams would toss the ball to a big center standing close to the basket who would toss in a hook shot or a layup. In those early years, the NBA was a "big man's league" dominated by such talented centers as George Mikan, Bill Russell, Wilt Chamberlain, and later Kareem Abdul-Jabbar and Shaquille O'Neal.

Mikan was so dominant underneath, the NBA changed the rules to make it harder for the big guys to score from close in. The league widened the restricted area near the basket—where players cannot stay for more than three seconds—from six feet to twelve feet in 1951. Later the NBA widened the three-second area, known as "the paint," to sixteen feet.

So good teams needed good shooters, players who could score from farther away from the basket. The Boston Celtics always had a great outside shooter during its run of eleven NBA championships

from 1957 to 1969. Bill Sharman was the first to fill the role. With his picture-perfect shooting form, Sharman led the NBA in foul shot percentage seven of his eleven seasons in the league.

Sam Jones took up the shooter's role after Sharman retired in 1961. The six-foot, four-inch guard often let go of his jump shot shouting "too late" to frustrated defenders. Another ball was in the bucket. Jones was part of ten Celtics championship teams, hitting more than 45 percent of his shots from the field and more than 80 percent of his free throws.

With the 24-second clock and a league full of fast-breaking, jump-shooting players, the scoreboards in the NBA were working overtime. During the 1961–62 season, every one of the nine NBA teams averaged more than 110 points a game. And that was before the three-point basket!

Since the 1960s, the scoring in the league has gone up and down, but the list of great NBA shooters is long.

Ray Allen . . . Larry Bird . . . "Downtown" Freddie Brown . . . Reggie Miller . . . Steve Nash . . . Dirk Nowitzki. And many more.

Now, with the three-point shot such a big part of every game, the NBA is a shooter's paradise. Players are sending up shots from all over the court. And nobody uses the two-hand set shot anymore.

The best of them all is Stephen Curry of the Golden State Warriors. The slender, baby-faced point guard may be the greatest outside shooter in the history of the NBA.

As Steve Nash, a pretty good shooter himself, observed, "Steph has taken things to a crazy, new place. Steph is not just stepping back, he's stepping back from three-point distance into never-never land. We've never seen that before, and we've certainly never seen anyone do it with that accuracy. What we're seeing is a revolution."

Curry is not alone. On his own team, Klay Thompson can put it up from just about anywhere, as well as superstar forward Kevin Durant. The Warriors rode their outside shooting and their "small ball" game—they often played without a true center—to three championships in four years (2015 to 2018).

So now almost everyone in the NBA is getting into the outside shooting act. Guards such as James Harden, J.J. Redick, Damian Lillard, and Buddy Hield are firing up as many as a dozen shots from downtown a game.

Even big men, such as Karl-Anthony Towns, Joel Embiid, and Kristaps Porziņģis, who in the old days would be hanging around the basket, are stepping back and firing long jumpers.

With so many sure shots, the scoreboards around the NBA are working overtime again. During the 2020–21 season, twenty-one of the thirty NBA teams averaged more than 110 points a game.

Harden has the ball on the left. He fakes a drive. Steps back. Three pointer. Good!

AT THE BUZZER

The arenas are filling up again following the worldwide coronavirus pandemic. The NBA has:

- State-of-the-art entertainment palaces such as the Chase Center in San Francisco, which fills four city blocks, seats eighteen-thousand fans, and features a huge scoreboard that is 9,600 square feet. The locker rooms at the Chase Center include wide-screen TVs and spacious individual areas for the players. A long way from the old Boston Garden, where early Celtic legends hung their clothes on a single hook nailed into the wall.
- An eighty-two game regular season, followed by four rounds of best-of-seven playoffs, when the action on the hardcourt really gets intense.
- Thirty franchises in thirty of the biggest cities in the United States and Canada, where fans root for their favorite teams and players. Fans all around the globe tune in by television and on every imaginable electronic device to follow the action.

Basketball, the game invented by James Naismith so many years ago, has grown into one of the most popular sports on the planet. And the NBA . . . is the biggest star in the basketball galaxy.

Maybe the game is so popular because it's so simple. All you need is a ball, a basket, a decent pair of shoes, and the desire to be the best you can be.

And maybe that's why so many different kinds of people (and future NBA stars) have fallen in love with the game over the years.

George Mikan was cut from his high school freshman team because he wore glasses and his coach thought he was too tall. He became a star in college by practicing one hundred right-handed and one hundred left-handed hook shots every day. Mikan later became the earliest NBA superstar and proved that big men could play the game.

Bob Cousy started playing basketball on the streets of New York to escape his parents' rocky marriage and a troubled home. His fancy passes made him "The Houdini of the Hardwood."

Bill Russell barely made his high school junior varsity team, but grew to change the NBA with his defense, rebounding, and unending desire to win. Russell won more NBA rings (eleven) than he had fingers to wear them.

Jerry West once said when recalling his rural West Virginia boyhood, "I think I became a basketball player because it is a game a boy can play by himself." He became the model for the logo of the NBA.

Bill Bradley, the only son of a Missouri banker, made himself into a basketball star at Princeton and for the New York Knicks through constant practice and constant movement on the court. He later became a United States Senator from New Jersey.

Scottie Pippen was one of twelve children. He grew seven inches at the University of Central Arkansas and later became a six-time NBA champion on the Chicago Bulls with Michael Jordan.

LeBron James was the only child of a single mom in Akron, Ohio. As a kid, James moved so often he missed eighty days of school in the fourth grade. He found a whole new group of friends by playing basketball on his youth and high school teams and then stardom in the NBA.

Stephen Curry was the son of a sixteen-season NBA player (Dell Curry). But this skinny guard for the Golden State Warriors grew up to be a better shooter than his dad . . . or maybe anyone in NBA history.

The players keep coming. From every corner of the earth and every imaginable background. Finding the game. Naismith's simple game. Trying to get better. Practicing and dreaming of playing in the biggest and best basketball league in the world.

The NBA.

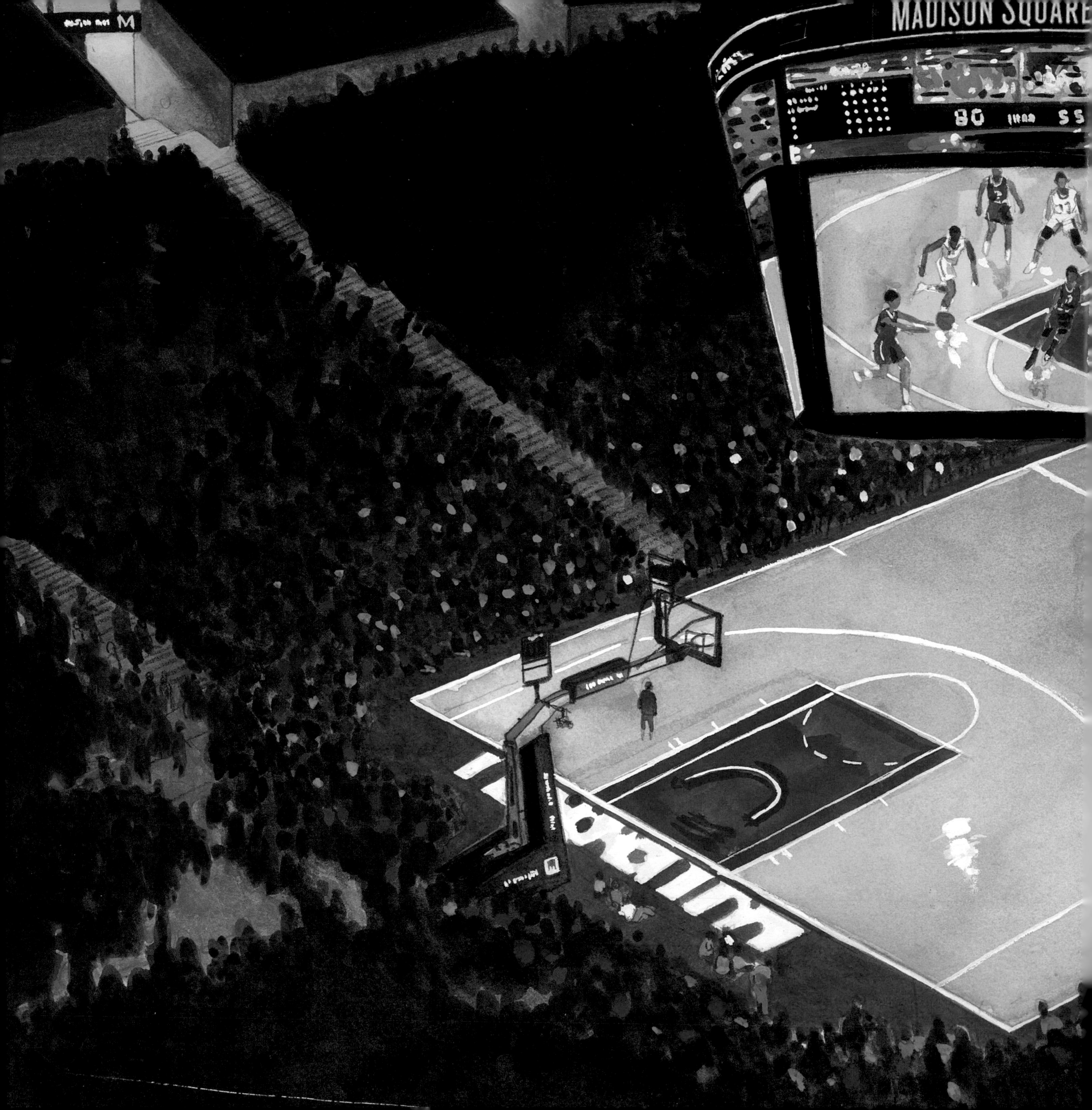

MADISON SQUARE
80
55

LIST OF NBA FINALS CHAMPIONS

(THROUGH 2021)

Year	Champion	Finals MVP (since 1969)	Runner-Up	Result
1947	**PHILADELPHIA WARRIORS**		*Chicago Stags*	4–1
1948	**BALTIMORE BULLETS**		*Philadelphia Warriors*	4–2
1949	**MINNEAPOLIS LAKERS**		*Washington Capitals*	4–2
1950	**MINNEAPOLIS LAKERS (2)**		*Syracuse Nationals*	4–2
1951	**ROCHESTER ROYALS**		*New York Knicks*	4–3
1952	**MINNEAPOLIS LAKERS (3)**		*New York Knicks*	4–3
1953	**MINNEAPOLIS LAKERS (4)**		*New York Knicks*	4–1
1954	**MINNEAPOLIS LAKERS (5)**		*Syracuse Nationals*	4–3
1955	**SYRACUSE NATIONALS**		*Fort Wayne Pistons*	4–3
1956	**PHILADELPHIA WARRIORS (2)**		*Fort Wayne Pistons*	4–1
1957	**BOSTON CELTICS**		*St. Louis Hawks*	4–3
1958	**ST. LOUIS HAWKS**		*Boston Celtics*	4–2
1959	**BOSTON CELTICS (2)**		*Minneapolis Lakers*	4–0
1960	**BOSTON CELTICS (3)**		*St. Louis Hawks*	4–3
1961	**BOSTON CELTICS (4)**		*St. Louis Hawks*	4–1
1962	**BOSTON CELTICS (5)**		*Los Angeles Lakers**	4–3
1963	**BOSTON CELTICS (6)**		*Los Angeles Lakers*	4–2
1964	**BOSTON CELTICS (7)**		*San Francisco Warriors***	4–1
1965	**BOSTON CELTICS (8)**		*Los Angeles Lakers*	4–1
1966	**BOSTON CELTICS (9)**		*Los Angeles Lakers*	4–3
1967	**PHILADELPHIA 76ERS (2)***		*San Francisco Warriors*	4–2
1968	**BOSTON CELTICS (10)**		*Los Angeles Lakers*	4–2
1969	**BOSTON CELTICS (11)**	Jerry West	*Los Angeles Lakers*	4–3
1970	**NEW YORK KNICKS**	Willis Reed	*Los Angeles Lakers*	4–3
1971	**MILWAUKEE BUCKS**	Kareem Abdul-Jabbar	*Baltimore Bullets*	4–0
1972	**LOS ANGELES LAKERS (6)**	Wilt Chamberlain	*New York Knicks*	4–1
1973	**NEW YORK KNICKS (2)**	Willis Reed (2)	*Los Angeles Lakers*	4–1
1974	**BOSTON CELTICS (12)**	John Havlicek	*Milwaukee Bucks*	4–3
1975	**GOLDEN STATE WARRIORS (3)**	Rick Barry	*Washington Bullets*	4–0
1976	**BOSTON CELTICS (13)**	Jo Jo White	*Phoenix Suns*	4–2
1977	**PORTLAND TRAIL BLAZERS**	Bill Walton	*Philadelphia 76ers***	4–2
1978	**WASHINGTON BULLETS**	Wes Unseld	*Seattle SuperSonics*	4–3

*In 1960, the Minneapolis Lakers became the Los Angeles Lakers. **In 1962, the Philadelphia Warriors became the San Francisco Warriors. In 1971, they became the Golden State Warriors. ***In 1963, the Syracuse Nationals became the Philadephia 76ers.

1979	**SEATTLE SUPERSONICS**	Dennis Johnson	*Washington Bullets*	4–1
1980	**LOS ANGELES LAKERS (7)**	Magic Johnson	*Philadelphia 76ers*	4–2
1981	**BOSTON CELTICS (14)**	Cedric Maxwell	*Houston Rockets*	4–2
1982	**LOS ANGELES LAKERS (8)**	Magic Johnson (2)	*Philadelphia 76ers*	4–2
1983	**PHILADELPHIA 76ERS (3)**	Moses Malone	*Los Angeles Lakers*	4–0
1984	**BOSTON CELTICS (15)**	Larry Bird	*Los Angeles Lakers*	4–3
1985	**LOS ANGELES LAKERS (9)**	Kareem Abdul-Jabbar (2)	*Boston Celtics*	4–2
1986	**BOSTON CELTICS (16)**	Larry Bird (2)	*Houston Rockets*	4–2
1987	**LOS ANGELES LAKERS (10)**	Magic Johnson (3)	*Boston Celtics*	4–2
1988	**LOS ANGELES LAKERS (11)**	James Worthy	*Detroit Pistons*	4–3
1989	**DETROIT PISTONS**	Joe Dumars	*Los Angeles Lakers*	4–0
1990	**DETROIT PISTONS (2)**	Isiah Thomas	*Portland Trail Blazers*	4–1
1991	**CHICAGO BULLS**	Michael Jordan	*Los Angeles Lakers*	4–1
1992	**CHICAGO BULLS (2)**	Michael Jordan (2)	*Portland Trail Blazers*	4–2
1993	**CHICAGO BULLS (3)**	Michael Jordan (3)	*Phoenix Suns*	4–2
1994	**HOUSTON ROCKETS**	Hakeem Olajuwon	*New York Knicks*	4–3
1995	**HOUSTON ROCKETS (2)**	Hakeem Olajuwon (2)	*Orlando Magic*	4–0
1996	**CHICAGO BULLS (4)**	Michael Jordan (4)	*Seattle SuperSonics*	4–2
1997	**CHICAGO BULLS (5)**	Michael Jordan (5)	*Utah Jazz*	4–2
1998	**CHICAGO BULLS (6)**	Michael Jordan (6)	*Utah Jazz*	4–2
1999	**SAN ANTONIO SPURS**	Tim Duncan	*New York Knicks*	4–1
2000	**LOS ANGELES LAKERS (12)**	Shaquille O'Neal	*Indiana Pacers*	4–2
2001	**LOS ANGELES LAKERS (13)**	Shaquille O'Neal (2)	*Philadelphia 76ers*	4–1
2002	**LOS ANGELES LAKERS (14)**	Shaquille O'Neal (3)	*New Jersey Nets*	4–0
2003	**SAN ANTONIO SPURS (2)**	Tim Duncan (2)	*New Jersey Nets*	4–2
2004	**DETROIT PISTONS (3)**	Chauncey Billups	*Los Angeles Lakers*	4–1
2005	**SAN ANTONIO SPURS (3)**	Tim Duncan (3)	*Detroit Pistons*	4–3
2006	**MIAMI HEAT**	Dwayne Wade	*Dallas Mavericks*	4–2
2007	**SAN ANTONIO SPURS (4)**	Tony Parker	*Cleveland Cavaliers*	4–0
2008	**BOSTON CELTICS (17)**	Paul Pierce	*Los Angeles Lakers*	4–2
2009	**LOS ANGELES LAKERS (15)**	Kobe Bryant	*Orlando Magic*	4–1
2010	**LOS ANGELES LAKERS (16)**	Kobe Bryant (2)	*Boston Celtics*	4–3
2011	**DALLAS MAVERICKS**	Dirk Nowitzki	*Miami Heat*	4–2
2012	**MIAMI HEAT (2)**	LeBron James	*Oklahoma City Thunder*	4–1
2013	**MIAMI HEAT (3)**	LeBron James (2)	*San Antonio Spurs*	4–3
2014	**SAN ANTONIO SPURS (5)**	Kawhi Leonard	*Miami Heat*	4–1
2015	**GOLDEN STATE WARRIORS (4)**	Andre Iguodala	*Cleveland Cavaliers*	4–2
2016	**CLEVELAND CAVALIERS**	LeBron James (3)	*Golden State Warriors***	4–3
2017	**GOLDEN STATE WARRIORS (5)**	Kevin Durant	*Cleveland Cavaliers*	4–1
2018	**GOLDEN STATE WARRIORS (6)**	Kevin Durant (2)	*Cleveland Cavaliers*	4–0
2019	**TORONTO RAPTORS**	Kawhi Leonard (2)	*Golden State Warriors*	4–2
2020	**LOS ANGELES LAKERS (17)**	LeBron James (4)	*Miami Heat*	4–2
2021	**MILWAUKEE BUCKS (2)**	Giannis Antetokounmpo	*Phoenix Suns*	4–2

CURRENT NBA FRANCHISES

(THROUGH 2021)

Current Team	Joined	Previous Team Names
Boston Celtics	1946	
New York Knicks	1946	
Golden State Warriors	1946	Philadelphia Warriors, San Francisco Warriors
Sacramento Kings	1948	Rochester Royals, Cincinnati Royals, Kansas City-Omaha Kings, Kansas City Kings
Los Angeles Lakers	1948	Minneapolis Lakers
Detroit Pistons	1948	Fort Wayne Pistons
Atlanta Hawks	1949	Tri-Cities Blackhawks, Milwaukee Hawks, St. Louis Hawks
Philadelphia 76ers	1949	Syracuse Nationals
Washington Wizards	1961	Chicago Packers, Chicago Zephyrs, Baltimore Bullets, Capital Bullets, Washington Bullets
Chicago Bulls	1966	
Houston Rockets	1967	San Diego Rockets
Oklahoma City Thunder	1967	Seattle SuperSonics
Milwaukee Bucks	1968	
Phoenix Suns	1968	
Cleveland Cavaliers	1970	
Los Angeles Clippers	1970	Buffalo Braves, San Diego Clippers
Portland Trail Blazers	1970	
Utah Jazz	1974	New Orleans Jazz
Brooklyn Nets	1976	New York Nets, New Jersey Nets
Denver Nuggets	1976	
Indiana Pacers	1976	
San Antonio Spurs	1976	
Dallas Mavericks	1980	
Miami Heat	1988	
Charlotte Hornets	1988	Charlotte Bobcats
Orlando Magic	1989	
Minnesota Timberwolves	1989	
Memphis Grizzlies	1995	Vancouver Grizzlies
Toronto Raptors	1995	
New Orleans Pelicans	2002	New Orleans Hornets, New Orleans/Oklahoma City Hornets

LIST OF NBA/ABA CAREER SCORING LEADERS

(REGULAR SEASON ONLY, THROUGH 2021)

Rank	Player	Teams	Points
1	Kareem Abdul-Jabbar	Bucks, Lakers	38,387
2	Karl Malone	Jazz, Lakers	36,928
3	LeBron James	Cavaliers, Heat, Lakers	35,367
4	Kobe Bryant	Lakers	33,643
5	Michael Jordan	Bulls, Wizards	32,292
6	Dirk Nowitzki	Mavericks	31,560
7	Wilt Chamberlain	Warriors, 76ers, Lakers	31,419
8	Julius Erving	Squires, Nets, 76ers	30,026
9	Moses Malone	Stars, Spirits, Braves, Rockets, 76ers, Bullets, Hawks, Bucks, Spurs	29,580
10	Shaquille O'Neal	Magic, Lakers, Heat, Suns, Cavaliers, Celtics	28,596
11	Dan Issel	Colonels, Nuggets	27,482
12	Carmelo Anthony	Nuggets, Knicks, Thunder, Rockets, Trail Blazers	27,370
13	Elvin Hayes	Rockets, Bullets	27,313
14	Hakeem Olajuwon	Rockets, Raptors	26,946
15	Oscar Robertson	Royals, Bucks	26,710
16	Dominique Wilkins	Hawks, Clippers, Celtics, Spurs, Magic	26,668
17	George Gervin	Squires, Spurs, Bulls	26,595
18	Tim Duncan	Spurs	26,496
19	Paul Pierce	Celtics, Nets, Wizards, Clippers	26,397
20	John Havlicek	Celtics	26,395
21	Kevin Garnett	Timberwolves, Celtics, Nets	26,071
22	Vince Carter	Raptors, Nets, Magic, Suns, Mavericks, Grizzlies, Kings, Hawks	25,728
23	Alex English	Bucks, Pacers, Nuggets, Mavericks	25,613
24	Reggie Miller	Pacers	25,279
24	Rick Barry	Warriors, Oaks, Capitols, Nets, Rockets	25,279
26	Jerry West	Lakers	25,192
27	Artis Gilmore	Colonels, Bulls, Spurs, Celtics	24,941
28	Patrick Ewing	Knicks, SuperSonics, Magic	24,815
29	Ray Allen	Bucks, SuperSonics, Celtics, Heat	24,505
30	Allen Iverson	76ers, Nuggets, Pistons, Grizzlies	24,368

INDEX

BIBLIOGRAPHY

BOOKS

Abrams, Jonathan. *Boys Among Men: How the Prep-to-Pro Generation Redefined the NBA and Sparked a Basketball Revolution*, 2016.

Araton, Harvey. *When the Garden was Eden: Clyde, the Captain, Dollar Bill and the Glory Days of the New York Knicks*, 2012.

Auerbach, Red and John Feinstein. *Let Me Tell You a Story: A Lifetime in the Game*, 2004.

Axthelm, Pete. *The City Game*, 1999.

Bird, Larry, Earvin Magic Johnson with Jackie MacMullan. *When the Game Was Ours*, 2009.

Fury, Shawn. *Rise and Fire: The Origins, Science and Evolution of the Jump Shot—And How It Transformed Basketball Forever*, 2017.

Grange, Michael. *Basketball's Greatest Stars* (Revised and Expanded) (2013 edition)

Halberstam, David. *Playing for Keeps: Michael Jordan and the World He Made*, 1999

Hareas, John. *Ultimate Basketball: More Than 100 Years of the Sport's Evolution*, 2004

LaBlanc, Michael L, editor. *Professional Sports Team Histories: Basketball*, 1994.

MacMullan, Jackie, Rafe Bartholomew and Dan Klores. *Basketball: A Love Story*, 2018

McCallum, Jack. *Dream Team: How Michael, Magic, Larry, Charles and the Greatest Team of All Time Conquered the World and Changed the Game of Basketball Forever*, 2012.

McCallum, Jack. *Golden Days: West's Lakers, Steph's Warriors and the California Dreamers Who Reinvented Basketball*, 2017.

Pluto, Terry. Loose Balls: *The Short, Wild Life of the American Basketball Association*, 2007.

Pluto, Terry. *Tall Tales: The Glory Years of the NBA, in the Words of the Men Who Played, Coached, and Built Pro Basketball*, 1992.

Pomerantz, Gary M. Wilt. *1962: The Night of 100 Points and the Dawn of a New Era*, 2006.

Pomerantz, Gary M. *The Last Pass: Cousy, Russell, the Celtics and What Matters in the End*, 2018.

Simmons, Bill. *The Book of Basketball: The NBA According to the Sports Guy*, 2009.

Spitz, Bob. *Shoot Out the Lights: The Amazing, Improbable, Exhilarating Saga of the 1969–70 New York Knicks*, 1995.

The Sporting News Official NBA Guide—1995–96 Edition

Thomas, Ron. *They Cleared the Lane: The NBA's Black Pioneers*, 2002.

ARTICLES

Badenhausen, Kurt. "How Michael Jordan Will Make $145 Million in 2019." *Forbes*, August 28, 2019.

Bamberger, Michael. "Everything You Always Wanted to Know about Free Throws . . . But Were Afraid to Ask Shaq." *Sports Illustrated*, April 13, 1998.

Christian, Scott. "Does Nike Really Sell 25 Pairs of Shoes per Second?" *Esquire*, October 12, 2016.

DeLessio, Joe. "Catching Up with New York Knicks Legend Dick Barnett." *Fordham News*, May 24, 2018.

Given, Karen. "NBA's Forgotten Co-Founder and the Shot Clock's True Origin Story." Wbur.org, *Only a Game* podcast transcript, April 7, 2017.

Goldstein, Richard. "In 1954, Shot Clock Revived a Stalled NBA." *New York Times*, December 25, 2004.

Sohi, Seerat. "How the NBA Was Saved on the Back of a Napkin." *SI.com*, August 28, 2017.

Thomas Jr., Robert McG. "Danny Biasone, Ex-Team Owner and NBA Innovator, Dies at 83." *New York Times*, May 27, 1992.

WEBSITES

allaboutbasketball.us—All About Basketball, Online Basketball Magazine

basketball-reference.com—NBA and ABA basketball statistics

sports-reference.com—information about college basketball

ESPN.com—website of the ESPN sports channel

NBA.com—information on the National Basketball Association

DOCUMENTARIES

Podhoretz, Jim, dir. *Celtics/Lakers: Best of Enemies*. An ESPN 30 for 30 Film, 2017.

Rapaport, Michael, dir. *When the Garden Was Eden*. An ESPN 30 for 30 Film, 2014.

DEDICATIONS

For Win and Rosanah Bennett—
good friends for a long time.   —F. B.

In Memory of Kobe Bean Bryant
(August 23, 1978–January 26, 2020)   —J. E. R.

ACKNOWLEDGMENTS

First and foremost, a big thanks goes to James Ransome for his fabulous artwork. I would also like to thank the folks at Margaret K. McElderry Books for all their support during this project. Finally, a shout-out to all the basketball writers listed in the bibliography. Their love of "Naismith ball" is a constant inspiration.